5 weeks to 5K

By Julie *"Fattymustrun"* Creffield

5 Weeks to 5K

Copyright: Julie Creffield

Published 1st April 2015

Publisher: The Fat Girls Guide to Running

The right of Julie Creffield to be identified as author of this Work has been asserted by her in accordance with sections 77 and 78 of the Copyright, Designs and Patents Act 1988. All rights reserved.

No part of this publication may be reproduced, stored in retrieval system, copied in any form or by any means, electronic, mechanical, photocopying, recording or otherwise transmitted without written permission from the publisher. You must not circulate this book in any format.

This book is licensed for your personal enjoyment only. This book may not be resold or given away to other people. If you would like to share this book with another person, please purchase an additional copy for each recipient.

Thank you for respecting the hard work of this author. Find out more about the author and upcoming books at www.toofatrun.co.uk or follow her on twitter @fattymustrun

Contents

So you want to run a 5K?..7
    Task 1 – Sign up to a 5K race 12
Week 1 - The Fear Factor 23
    Task 2 – The first attempt..27
    Task 3 – Letting it all out..28
    Task 4 – Play the "so what?" game 30
    Task 5 – Out and back for 12 32
    Task 6 – Out and back for 15 32
Week 2 – Assessing where you are..34
    Task 7 – Baseline Record 35
    Task 8 – The getaway 37
    Task 9 – How long can you last?...38
    Task 10 – Time on your feet test 39
Week 3 - Improving Technique 42
    Task 11 – Deep breathing practice..45
    Task 12 – Top to toe assessment 46
    Task 13 – Experimenting with speed.......................................49
Week 4 - Be Inspired..50
    Task 14 – Plot a new route..52
    Task 15 – Podcast/Audiobook Run 54
    Task 16 – Sightseeing Run 56
Week 5 – Believing you can do it 59
    Task 17 – What's the worst that can happen? 60
    Task 18 – Lets keep those legs loose (combine this with task 21) 62
    Task 19 – How does it feel?..62
    Task 20 - Give your legs a treat 63

Task 21 – Give us a fashion show...64
Race Day Preparation 64
Task 22 - Take a picture...68
Conclusion 70
Task 23 – Schedule your next run...71
Task 24 – Set some new goals 72
Task 25 – This is a little bit of a cheeky one…................................74
Check List 76
Acknowledgements 77

So you want to run a 5K?

It seems like everyone and their dog are running 5k races these days, donning their pink tutus or being covered in paint as they go; it is somewhat infectious. Maybe you have got caught up in this hype and are simply jumping on the bandwagon, wanting your moment of glory, or perhaps learning how to run really has been a burning desire you've had hidden inside you and it's just by coincidence that now you are 100% ready to tackle it.

Well I couldn't think of a better time to give it a go.

I can't remember when, as an adult, I initially thought about taking up the sport, as for me running was never something I had even considered. I didn't know any runners and, aside from a rather embarrassing moment in the Year 9 sports day, it had rarely featured in my life; it was just something that those other annoyingly fit (and usually much slimmer) people did to show off.

Secretly, and quite foolishly though, I did believe that I would easily be able to do it if I really wanted to, "yeah, I could run if I wanted to…I just don't want to that's all" was my attitude. I seriously kidded myself that without any effort or dedication on my part that I would be able to don some running shoes, squeeze into some Lycra and find my feet. Crazy hey? Especially considering at this time in my life, I was close to 5 stone overweight and not doing any formal exercise, unless you counted raving all weekend with my friends or carrying my frozen pizzas and multiple bottles of wine home from the supermarket.

So you can imagine what an almighty shock it was when at just 24 years of age I almost died running a 3k-community fun run in my neighborhood. OK so that is a slight exaggeration; I didn't nearly die but it seriously felt like I was going to at the time, both physically and emotionally. Firstly, I was not prepared for how hard it would be on my out of shape body, or equally how ashamed I would feel for being so obviously incapable at my age.

The realisation that my current body could not do what I wanted it to do and the fact that my partying lifestyle was taking such a tremendous toll on my health was just the wake up call I needed though, and I embarked on a challenge to complete in the 2006 London Triathlon…a swim, a cycle and a run.

I don't do things by halves.

I was like a women on a mission, signing up for adult swimming classes to learn how to do front crawl properly, buying a cheap catalogue bike so I could cycle back and forward to work…and of course the run? Well we all know how to run right?

I never did get round to the running part of the training so its no wonder that on the day of the event after my 400 meter swim in the docks and my 10K cycle in the midday heat I was completely incapable of running the 2.5k final leg of this monumental event….and I had to make do with powerwalking….or as I remember it back then: the walk of shame.

I was still a good size 18 at this point and the thought of me running around London's Docklands in my wetsuit still gives me nightmares, but the point is despite not running more than a few 30 second bursts including an impressive sprint finish I still completed the race…I SIMPLY HAD TO COMPLETE THE RACE!!

As a result of that first disastrous 3-kilometer running event just 3 months prior I had set myself up in such a way for this one that I could not fail. I had committed fully to the event; I had trained for it (well kind of); I had told the whole world about it, meaning the bulk of my family were there to support me on the day…could you imagine how embarrassing it would have been to pull out at any point? NO. Failure was never an option. I had something to prove to myself and more importantly I had some unfinished business with this body of mine.

The moment I crossed under that finishing gantry and held the medal in my hands for a picture I realised that I could achieve things, I wouldn't be laughed at…even in my still out of shape and some what unsightly body. I simply had to believe I could do it and take enough small steps towards achieving that goal that eventually it happens.

Looking back though, I still wish I had run more of the run leg…it felt humiliating having everyone basking in the summer sun, drinking beer along the course with me powerwalking with a beetroot red face surrounded by thousands of "proper" competitors. If only I had scheduled regular runs into my week, if only I had followed a proper programme like everyone had suggested, if only I had faced my absolute dreadful fear of running…perhaps I would have enjoyed it more.

But nether the less the London Triathlon marked the start of my 10 year love hate relationship with running and this book serves to prevent you from spending a whole decade fighting an unnecessary, and at times soul destroying, battle to discover the joy of this sport…you guys get to do that in just 5 weeks.

Yes that's right, I reckon I can help you learn to the love the sport of running in just 5 weeks.

So what should you expect to find in this book?

5 weeks to 5k is a simple running guide to get you running the popular 5K distance as quickly as possible with as little fuss as necessary. There will be no "you must run on this day, and you must fuel yourself this way" Because, come on ladies, we have exciting lives to lead outside of any running ambitions right? Plus nobody likes being told what to do.

Well I don't.

So please don't expect any unnecessary talk of sports bras and the value in getting properly fitted running shoes, or detail about the best stretches to do after a long run…that's what the internet is for (well it is for me) so get researching…a good place to start is www.toofattorun.co.uk for loads of free advice on getting started.

No.

This book is taking you back to basics, giving you a friendly boot out the front door each week whilst talking you through the possible problems you may encounter along the way. The goal is to get you to the 5K point without you having a nervous breakdown, hitting the hubby over the head with a brick or having a pity party for one in the process.

You will find this book simple to follow, no jargon to confuse you no difficult plan to squeeze into your schedule. Just read it week by week and complete each of the weekly tasks in order.

Seriously guys, I know its tempting to read a book cover to cover to get a feel for what lies ahead but I think you are more likely to be successful over the next 5 weeks if you simply put the book down each time there is a new task to complete and only pick it up again once you have ticked it off your list.

So lets start off how we mean to go on with your first challenge of the book. See if you can resist the urge to read on and trust that I know what I am doing.

Task 1 – Sign up to a 5K race

When you have an immovable date in the diary, a goal to work towards you are more likely to follow a programme and find the motivation needed to get you off the couch, even if that is through fear of looking silly come race day. So find a 5K event 5 weeks from now, or schedule your own event and let everyone know that you have done it. "I am running a 5k race on…" whatever the date is, is far more impressive than "oh I've started up running, and I'm supposed to be ready for a 5K in just 5 weeks" don't you think?

To help you feel like you are working the programme there is a summary of the 5-week plan in the form of a checklist, which can be found at the end of the book to be printed out and stuck to your fridge, or you can download a 5 week planner from www.toofattorun.co.uk/shop

Why not increase your accountability by joining our friendly Facebook page www.facebook.com/thefatgirlsguidetorunning where you can discuss your progress and get support from other women just like you?

Or if you really need some hand holding why not sign up to our quarterly 5 weeks to 5k online programmes where you can follow the principles of this book along with a group of like minded women, with weekly video coaching sessions, mindset tasks and a closed Facebook page to share progress. Check out www.toofattorun.co.uk for details of how to register.

I believe you can do this, the question is do you? Even if you are not 100% sure you can right now that's OK, but all I ask is you commit to going out 3 times a week for the following 5 weeks, that you give the challenges a go to the best of your ability and of course try to enjoy the whole process…because after all this running malarkey is supposed to be fun too…well that's what all those funky sports adverts would have you believe.

But why Running?

Running is such a popular sport for women these days, perhaps due to its flexibility for complementing your lifestyle and of course its ever luring promise of weight loss, but for every women that successfully learns to run there are scores of women that continue to battle with it as a sport, frustrated at its apparent difficulty or annoyed at their failure to see improvement…and then of course there are the women who don't even entertain the idea of running at all, perhaps believing that it is easier not to try than to try and fail right?

Wrong.

With running you can't really fail. You have already learned how to run once so chances are you can do it again, so what have you got to lose? Perhaps this is about how you are setting this all up in your head.

As human beings, most of us have been running at pace from about the age of 2 so we should pretty much all be able to do it by now, yes even YOU and the thing is we can.... all of us. However, what we often fail to acknowledge is that despite having the same anatomical bits and bobs as each other we are all built quite differently and are definitely motivated in different ways.

So I believe the sport of running has to be introduced at a rate that is personally right for you and not with a one size fits all approach; you have to listen to your own signals and tackle it on your own terms...if of course you want to get to grips with it once and for all.

At this stage you might be thinking that's all well and good but I can't even run for a bus, or maybe you know you can ran but you can only last for about 30 seconds at a time before having to stop and walk, but chances are for majority of you reading this book even now at some points in your current life you do actually run. You just don't realise you are doing it.

Whether its to catch a flight you are late for, or to save a disaster like an overflowing bath...the point is when we really need to run we can and we do, the trick now though is to work out how to sustain it for much longer periods of time and to find a way of making it an integral part of your life.

I guess this is as good a point as any to make the announcement that I am not particularly a huge fan of the well-known beginner running programme that is Couch to 5K.

Yep: SHOCK HORROR!

My main gripe for this popular programme with its downloadable guides, mobile phone apps, podcasts and even local beginners running projects following its principles is that it can often appear that the 5K point in the programme is some kind of end point like once you have achieved that then you have really cracked it and then, and only then can you start calling yourself a runner.

But what if you don't get to the point of being to run a 5k without stopping, have you not succeeded? Should you just give up and try something else? Or maybe you should just go back to start week 1 of the programme all over again and give it another shot…urrrggghhh talk about demotivating.

Isn't that system of progressing only when you have reached a certain standard setting you up for failure or more importantly mind numbing boredom? All that focusing on how much you have to run each time? Clock watching and sticking to THE PLAN? It's enough to turn anyone off of running for life.

Many beginners' programmes assume that we are all the same; that we will all progress at a similar speed to one other and that our capacity to motivate ourselves fits within their rigid timeframe. And I am much too much of a maverick to believe one size fits all, especially when it comes to women.

For example most beginners programmes suggest that you can go from zero to 5K in about 12 weeks, with gentle weekly progression in distance and time on your feet split up into different sessions. But what about actually listening to your body? How about running when you feel like it, or when it suits what else is going on in your life. Do you really want to follow a plan that tells you to walk when you could quite easily carry on and run further? Or similarly a plan which insists you should run when your legs are still very sore from the previous session?

But granted, I do accept that millions of women around the world have successfully used the Couch to 5K system to get them started, so instead of slagging it off completely and saying it doesn't work (because for many women it does) I would simply suggest that my 5 weeks to 5k system is an alternative method to try, one which bravely goes where no other programme goes…well none I have ever seen anyway.

But before we get into the nitty gritty I thought I would give you a simple overview of how to run (for those of you still not sure). In my first eBook

'Getting Past the First 30 Seconds' I broke down the main 5 problems we face as beginners

1. Being physically unfit
2. Starting off too fast
3. Not breathing properly
4. Caring too much about what other people think
5. Listening to the voices in your head

This book will touch on all of these but in particular it focuses on the "Voices in the head" one, because I truly believe that it is our minds that let us down not our bodies when it comes to playing sport, particularly if we have body confidence issues or are overweight or unfit. If only we could train our mindset and our will to succeed alongside our legs chances are we would become unstoppable.

So 5 things to remember each time you run (and you can write them on your fingers if you need a reminder) that will really help you to run more easily

1. Your current fitness is affecting the effort you need to put in, but it will get easier.
2. SLOW RIGHT DOWN if you want to run for longer periods of time.
3. Control your breathing, in through your nose and out through your mouth.
4. Care less about what others think. This is your thing, don't let them ruin it for you.
5. Ignore the negative voices in your own head; you can do this!

Remember ladies, running is simply a matter of putting one foot in front of another and repeating, for you this might be at walking pace and for others there may actually be a gap under their feet as they move along at speed. But lets not focus on that for now, you will find where you are at pace wise as you build in confidence but the most important thing now is starting to think like a runner…like an athlete in fact.

And you had better do this quick, because we have a 5K run to train for don't you know?

Is it really possible to do this in only 5 weeks though?

I am sure you have all heard horror stories about people taking up a new sport and doing themselves an injury in the first few weeks, so of course you are right to have some concerns about the impact of this new activity on your body. After all, running has a terribly reputation for damaging joints, and then there are all those people who end up in ditches with twisted ankles.

But this is all about risk and managing that risk.

Some Doctors and fitness experts might say that going from nothing to 5K in just 5 weeks is dangerous, but I would argue that most of us cover the 5K distance each weekend as we trudge around shopping centers loaded up with our purchases, so how is this any different

When I talk about getting you to run a 5K I am not necessarily expecting every single one of you to be able to complete the distance in a great time (whatever that is) and without stopping for the occasional walking break. However, I truly believe that if you put on your running shoes and head out the door to complete a 5K then it doesn't matter if you walk, jog or run it…it still constitutes the running a 5K…but then maybe I am bias, in my books anyone who thinks like an athlete, and trains like an athlete in the lead up to their big event…well they should be congratulated for their efforts just like any other athlete.

The reason that the 5 weeks to 5k programme is so successful is that it encourages you to listen to your body, working with it rather than against it, therefore there is no greater risk in starting this programme than there is to happening upon a steep hill on holiday, or discovering the lifts are broken in your office block.

If you have existing health problems or are particularly anxious about increasing your activity then of course go and talk to your GP, tell him that you are going to be committing to 3 lots of 30 minutes of gentle to moderate exercise each week for 5 weeks using a programme that encourages you to work within your limits to improve your confidence, fitness and mental health. I'd be interested to see what they can object to, because 3x30 is the governments physical activity targets and surely GPs want you to meet those targets right?

But what is the purpose in speeding up this process, why not take the 12 weeks to get there, what's the rush to get to that all important 5K you may be thinking?

Well, from my experience of supporting women to take up exercise I find that for you to keep interested in a new activity you have to see at least some tangible progress in the first few weeks, you have to feel like you are challenging yourself and you have to believe that the goal is worth working hard for in the first place…and if you are going to take 3 months to get to that point maybe the goal doesn't seem worth it after all.

Or maybe I am simply too impatient for my own good.

My first official race after the disastrous 3k, and the ever so dramatic Triathlon was a 10K, the British 10K in Central London…so lets just think about that for a moment. I struggled at 3K, failed completely at 2.5k and still thought it was a good idea to go right up to a 10K distance.

Was I scared…of course I was, but I channeled that nervous energy into my training and managed to run about 50-60% of that race, all off the back of about 8 weeks training. But why set myself such a big target? Possibly to make up for being so rubbish at the shorter distances…I wanted to prove that I could do it…and ultimately I did.

So you see I already believe you can cover the 5k distance, even now…even from your starting point of not being a runner…or being a lapsed runner so now its just about speeding you up a bit and giving you the confidence to run rather than stroll. And I don't need more than 5 weeks to do that. So I really don't see it as a huge step for you to take physically, especially when the challenges in the programme are specifically designed to build you up to the distance safely. The challenge is about finding the mental strength needed to see it through.

And for that you will have to commit completely to it.

This commitment involves making an honest assessment of your ability to give up an hour and a half of your week to this challenge…consistently for 5 weeks, no gaps, no holidays, no excuses. Reckon you can do it?

This is about scheduling this into your busy lives. Prioritizing your health and fitness over and above the needs of your family or your crazy work schedule. Telling loved ones that you want to do this…that you need to do this, and that you will be expecting their support to enable you to do it. How often do you do things like this for yourself? Is now the time to start?

Of course it is, as I always say the best time to start running was actually two years ago, the second best time is today.

But you have to ask yourself quite honestly whether this is the absolute right time for you to start such a campaign? Would it be better delaying it until a time where you are less stressed or have more time to play around with? What else are you going through right now at work or in your relationships? Who else needs you? Can you give this project the focus that you need to? Can you do it justice? Or are we just looking at excuses again.

Remember ladies it is only 5 weeks out of your life…just 35 measly days…840 hours. You can commit to that right? Well let's go then. Put a firm date in your diary for getting started and lets do this.

Week 1 - The Fear Factor

In 2015 a Sport England study revealed that two million fewer women than men play sport regularly but surprisingly 75 per cent of the women surveyed admitted that they did want to be more active, but many of them said they were simply put off by fear.

You know what it's like: you stop doing sport at school, get on with your life as an adult and then realise for one reason or another you want to be more active or perhaps take up a sport. But it's tough as adult women, starting something new, in this body that all of a sudden we don't recognize.

Firstly, we have to think about the logistics of fitting the sport into our life, then there is the problem of finding somewhere to do it that doesn't cost the earth and takes beginners…and then just as we think we have got the green light the voices in our head start putting their two pence worth in. What if everyone there is better than me, more attractive than me, wears nicer kit, and weighs less…perhaps I'll just stick on a DVD at home hey and forget all about doing a proper activity for me.

Why as women are we so fearful? Why do we scupper our plans like that before we have even started?

The main things that women tend to be scared of as confirmed by the research are

1. What they looked like during exercise
2. Not being completely rubbish at the activity and feeling silly
3. Being judged for prioritizing my needs over the families/boyfriends/work commitments

Universal concerns hey?

Worst still is these fears are often magnified when it comes to those who most need to exercise. At what point in the process of gaining weight do you say, "OK enough is enough, I am heading down the gym", especially if you hate what you see in the mirror. The world is obsessed with our growing waistlines, and the so called obesity epidemic…and trust me, as someone who has spent most of her adult life dancing around the obese end of the BMI scale, I, of course, feel the pressure to conform.

But there has to be another way.

Shouldn't we be exercising because it's enjoyable, it boosts our self esteem and confidence, it makes us a happier and nicer citizen? Even if we don't lose a single pound, exercise is sure as hell, going to make us feel better about ourselves.

Millions of pounds of tax payers money is being invested in weight loss solutions; the diet and fitness industry is booming yet nobody seems to acknowledge the extent of that crippling fear that overweight women often have when it comes to exercise: "I don't want to run in public in case people laugh at me" being the most common complaint, or "I can't join a running club because I am too slow, and I would just get left behind or hold everyone else up."

I did some research of my own last year to explore the specific barriers to running for larger women, and by that I simply mean women who don't look like your average runner, as seen on the front of Women's Running or in the latest Nike advert. I have been working with overweight women for close to 5 years; much of what I understood about this niche was anecdotal but my interim findings unsurprisingly corresponded directly with the data from Sport England, with 76% of responders reporting that feeling self-conscious was the number 1 barrier to participation, followed by concerns about being too slow (56%) and then by finding kit that fits (48%).

Now these are all valid fears, and I have experienced all of them to my detriment, but come on ladies don't you think it's time we faced our fears? The lads don't feel as self conscious as we do, and if they do they don't show it. They just get on with whatever it is they want to get involved in, not giving a damn about what they look like, if they are at all rubbish or even if they are being selfish with their time…it's often their competitive spirit driving them on and for them its always about winning which is probably why so many more men play sport than us, oh that and the fact we too often get lumbered with the housework and the kids.

I remember so clearly when I first started running, not wanting to be seen by anyone, cringing every time a bus went past, or if there happened to be a bunch of teenagers in my path just in case they laughed at me or thought mean things about me, but I kept going out there facing those fears because my fear of just giving up and admitting defeat was even greater. I also had massive fears about entering races in case I was the slowest or the fattest, what would happen if I couldn't finish the event?

I still have fears when it comes to my running, even now after 10 years of being part of the sport, but now I identify what those fears are all about and manage them so that they don't get in the way of me achieving my goals. Over time, the fears become less of a problem even if they never completely disappear.

But you are at the start of this journey, so it's quite possible that your fears feel quite overwhelming. So many things to think about, so many things that could go wrong…and you don't want to commit to this if there is any likelihood that you can't complete it…but hang on a minute, we are getting a little ahead of ourselves here we just need to tackle things one at a time.

And first things first I am going to kick you out the front door to do the one thing you are most scared of right now…RUNNING IN PUBLIC. Today ladies we start your journey to becoming a 5K athlete with an actual run, in fact let me rephrase that YOU start your journey to becoming that person. You are going for a run.

Task 2 – The first attempt

Head out the door in your running gear (or whatever you feel comfortable in), travel for 10 whole minutes and then turn round and return home the way you came. Do not go to the gym, or run on a treadmill and whatever you do, please don't drive to a different neighborhood where nobody knows you, it's really important that you leave your own front door for this first run.

But hold up, you can't run for 20 minutes right?

That's OK because, for the purposes of this book, whenever I say the word run, you can interpret that however you like as long as you are moving….so you can walk, powerwalk, skip, jog, gallop or run or do a mixture of all of these…I really don't mind. So let me repeat that again for anyone worrying about having to be able to run to take part in this programme. When I say RUN what I actually mean is walk, jog or run whichever you are most comfortable with. I do of course want you to push yourself and work up a bit of a sweat, but start off slow and only increase the speed if you feel like your body can cope…and slow down again if it becomes too hard. The main thing is you get out for this first session so you have got it out of the way....one less things to worry about.

So what are you waiting for? Off you pop....Seriously come on. Do not read on any further in this book until you have returned home from your first out and back run. That is the technical term ladies 'Out and Back'. You know what to do.

Back already? Great. How did it feel? Was it as terrible as you thought it might be? Did you die of shame or embarrassment, or did your heart give up or your legs stop working under the strain?

Of course not, so well done. You can now consider yourself a runner.

Task 3 – Letting it all out

So now what? Well you know how us ladies like making lists? I want you to list all the things you are still scared of when it comes to running. Particularly what you are worried about in terms of getting to the 5K point. Yep…that's where we are going next as we can't face our fears unless we know what they all are.

Take a sheet of paper and give yourself twenty minutes or so to really explore what it is you are scared of. Just write it all down without editing yourself, if you think it scribble it down. Do it with a friend if this helps. Get them to ask why…but why…yes but why, until you get to the real crux of the problem, get to the underlying issue.

It might look a bit like this

I am afraid of

- Looking horrible in Lycra

- My neighbors seeing me
- Admitting I've let myself go
- Starting from scratch again
- Not being able to breathe
- Having to walk after a few seconds
- Looking all hot and sweaty

These are my fears even now after 10 years of running; I still feel them but perhaps just not as strongly as I once did. The fear of embarrassment, the fear of ridicule and the fear of being rubbish are not exclusive to big women of course, as these insecurities sadly live inside many of our heads regardless of our shape or size, but the good news is much of this negativity can be changed with a little bit of faith and determination on our part. So let's look at that list again and start breaking these down and finding solutions to minimize the fear…

Looking horrible in Lycra – Do I need to wear Lycra? Should I buy myself some nice new kit? Do I really look that bad anyway? Says who? Will running improve the way I look eventually? Will anyone out there really look at me anyway? Do I care what they think?

So you can see how I have taken a realistic common fear and started to unpack it. The fear in this case is being manifested in your own mind. So unlike some fears like falling off a cliff or encountering a spider…you are not actually in any danger, this is about something that you can control.

Lets try another one.

My neighbours seeing me – Will they? What is the likelihood? What if they do? What will they think? Really? What does that say about them? Do you not think they might be impressed?

Jealous? Inspired? Do you care what they think? Are you living your life for them or for you?

Don't get me wrong we all want to be liked and look good in front of people, me included but most of the time people are far more concerned about their own lives and how they look than other people, besides we are our own worse critics it probably isn't as bad as you imagine.

But when these voices appear (as they occasionally do) I always like to remember my favorite Mae West quote

"Better to be looked over than overlooked" the other phrase which comes into mind is "Stuff em" or words to that effect which are better left out of this book.

Task 4 – Play the "so what?" game

What I would like you to do now is to go through your list and smash those psychological fears to pieces in what I like to call the "so what game?" Tackle each fear, one by one, until you have really explored what it means for you to face that fear. I find having an attitude of "Well, what's the worst that could happen" really helps.

In 2014 I signed up for an event called Tough Mudder billed as the most grueling obstacle course on the planet. Why did I do such a thing? Well in truth I didn't really think it through and then once I had agreed to do it I found it hard to pull out. I am a runner but my upper body and general cardio fitness is actually quite poor, so I knew if I was going to complete this 12 mile course with its 22 horrendous challenges I would have to train and I did. But that didn't stop the fear. I was so scared in the lead up, worrying about whether I would get round, but that was nothing compared to the fear I felt on the day. Every single one of those obstacles scared the living daylights out of me, in fact before the race even started I faced my ultimate fear…being lifted by someone else, and that was just to get to the start line.

The fear was unlike anything I have ever felt, jumping off a 30ft platform into brown murky water, submerging myself in a skip full of ice, scaling a wall so high that once at the top I could feel it swaying in the wind….now this, my friends, is fear. The type of fear that rages through your body and that lasts in your bodies memory for ever more, even after you have conquered it.

Remind me what you are scared of again?

Task 5 – Out and back for 12

So now you have identified what your fears are and how you are going to think differently about them. Let's get back to the running. You have been out for one 'Out and Back' run already this week, but as promised you did say you would commit to 3 sessions a week so I would like you to revisit that fear of running of course with your new found coping strategies but for slightly longer. Head out for 12 minutes before turning round and making your way home, and make a mental note of how much harder it is to add those few extra minutes to your route.

Task 6 – Out and back for 15

This is the last session of the week and is much the same as the previous one. Head out again for 15 minutes before stopping and returning home. So lets get this right, that's 30 minutes of walk, run or jogging (whichever you and your body prefers) under your belt and look we are still only on week 1. When you arrive home and get your breath back I want you to somehow estimate the distance you have just travelled. You may have a snazzy watch, or a smart mobile phone app that will measure it for you, but an old skool map or the AA route finder website on the internet will do. Remember this doesn't need to be accurate, it just needs to give you an idea of what you have achieved in week 1.

So how are you feeling? Sore? Surprised at how hard or how easy it was, or even that you managed to stick to the plan and complete all 3 sessions? Well remember ladies this is just week 1 and perhaps you have, in the past, experienced the first flourish of enthusiasm for a new challenge, and there are 4 more weeks to go of course. We have to keep our motivation high and continue to commit to making our goal a reality.

But three sessions in a week to me signals that you have the aptitude to become a great runner…no seriously.

Week 2 – Assessing where you are

The easiest way to become a runner is simply to run. It's like the time I asked my Great Uncle Les a semi famous journalist how to become a writer, his simple response of "just write" was frustrating as an impatient 17 year old but now I completely understand where he was coming from. There is no magic or trickery involved in becoming a proper runner its simply about practice, doing it frequently enough for your body to get used to the idea.

So week two is all about creating a routine but also assessing where you are starting from so that you can set realistic goals for the future. When I think about the kind of ladies that will be reading this book, I know there is not just one type of woman, how could there be? We are all so different and when it comes to running, we all run for different reasons and start of from different starting points. Perhaps you have been a regular runner on the past and have just got out of the habit, perhaps you have just had a baby, perhaps you have never run or perhaps you have tried and failed many times before.

One of my biggest regrets, when I look back at the last 10 years, is not keeping a record of my achievements, so I could look back and review the data in a meaningful way. Of course I can take a look through my piles of race medals, and search through my old blog posts to remind myself of where I have come but there are certain measurables which I simply didn't measure….or if I did, I didn't note them down anywhere safe for me to review at a later date.

How can you know how far you have come if you don't know what you are judging it against, equally how can you set goals and know that they are realistic if you have no idea how steep the learning and improvement needs to be.

We will be exploring a range of issues this week, fitness, speed, endurance, mental strength but most of all the ability to simply stick to the plan and give everything a go. For every task you complete you are getting closer and closer to your goal. Just put one foot in front of the other and tick them off one by one.

Task 7 – Baseline Record

This week I want you to spend some time collating a baseline record. This will require you to get on the scales, use a measuring tape and dig out a stopwatch. You of course will be doing your 3 runs this week and adding data from that to this record but for now just think about the best way for you to record a range of different measurements. I have a snazzy document now stored on my desktop and it may be motivational for you to create your own, I have also used the notes section in my phone for this but for now a scribbled version on paper will be fine.

You have a week to basically record the following 25 required pieces of information

1. Height
2. Weight
3. BMI (Body Mass Index)
4. Chest Measurement
5. Waist Measurement
6. Hip Measurement
7. Thigh Measurement
8. Arm Measurement
9. Body Fat Percentage
10. Body Muscle
11. Body Water
12. How many hours of sleep you get on average per night

13. How much time per day you sit on your bum
14. How many hours of exercise do you do per week
15. How far (in minutes) can you run before you need to walk
16. Have you run a 5k how long did it take you
17. How far can you travel in 30 minutes
18. How do you feel in your running kit
19. How do you feel running in public
20. How confident are you to go into a running shop and ask for advice
21. How much water do you drink per day
22. How many portions of fruit and veg do you eat per day
23. How many units of alcohol do you consume per week
24. How many sugary/fat laded snacks do you eat per week
25. Do you smoke?

Now you may be getting a bit fearful or panicky about this, or perhaps you are rolling your eyes and thinking why on earth do I need to know all this stuff, especially as I am an advocate for doing exercise outside of any desire to lose weight. But weight loss is a focus for some people and inch loss can be aswell. Some of it may not be relevant for you but what these 25 indicators do for me is give a picture of the overall health and well being of a person, and more importantly gives me clues at to areas of their life where they can make improvements or simply minor adjustments.

The idea is that by storing this information at the start of your journey, just 7 or 8 days in, it gives you a marker to assess how far you have come when you reach your 5K goal in about 25 days or so. It also forces you to face the reality of where you are now, and sometimes that, in itself, is one of the biggest barriers. It can be one of the greatest motivators too, so this is all about mindset and having the tools to get you to where you want to be.

Task 8 – The getaway

How about a run now? Ever watched one of those challenges where contestants have 24 hours and no money to get as far away from a specific spot as possible, with the winner often managing to hitch a lift, or beg, borrow and steal to get as far up the M1 as they can before the times up? Well this task is a little bit like that but less dramatic. You have 30 minutes and you have to simply go as far as you can in that time. Of course you can create a loop so that it brings you back home, or one of my favorite ways of running is actually trying to run somewhere and then jumping on a bus home (or getting my sister to pick me up).

If picturing an army of zombies chasing you, or imagining you were trying to flee the scene of a crime helps, then go for it. But remember once again, when I say run what I am really meaning is travelling in its broadest sense…whether that be walk, jog or run…but obviously the more you run the further away you will get. But do listen to your body and don't go mad. When you get back home record the distance on your baseline record.

Task 9 – How long can you last?

Make sure you leave a day or two between the last session and this so that your legs are feeling relatively fresh, but hopefully the excitement of the how far can you run challenge will have illustrated that when you have a target to meet or you want to do as well as you can, well then you do push yourself.

But whereas the previous session was about speed, for this one I am going to ask you to completely slow things down. I want you to find a pace where seriously you could walk faster, but I would like you to try and run, so that will involve the swinging of you arms a slight bounce in your step and at least the illusion that you are running.

The aim of this session is for you to see how long you can sustain this, so after a light warm up…some squats, some running on the spot, some general loosening up of your joints, I want you to set off and try to keep going for as long as you can. For this task, you are going to have to summon all of your physical strength but more importantly your mental strength, your capacity to keep going when the voices in your head want you to stop.

You should limit the session to only 30 minutes, but depending on how long your longest burst of running is, you can try this a number of times to see if you can extend it. So for example if the first attempt results in only 90 seconds then that is fine, do a bit of powerwalking think about what it was that really made you stop and give it another go….but it you manage a 20 minute burst then give yourself a pat on the back and head home.

Task 10 – Time on your feet test

So with two pretty tough running sessions already under your belt this week, you might think I would let up on you and give you a nice easy session. Do ya reckon?

When you get to run your 5K in what is now just 3 weeks away whether you walk, jog or run the distance you can already start to do the maths in terms of how long it will take you to get around the distance.

My first official 5K was on Wimbledon Common as part of an organized weekly running event known as parkrun (if you haven't heard of www.parkrun.com you really should check them out), I didn't know how long it should take me to get round or how speedy the other runners would be but I set off and gave it my best shot coming in with a grand old finishing time of 37 minutes and 28 seconds. I bet you are already thinking about how fast you will run it and perhaps are worrying that it won't be anywhere near my time. Why would it be? You are not me and why would you want to compare yourself to me for anyway. This is about your journey.

I went to that first parkrun off the back of a week long fitness bootcamp, so was in reasonable fitness shape despite my size 20 frame, and I was fired up about making exercise a big part of my life. If I had run that event 3 weeks prior though, it's likely it would have taken me close to an hour.

The point I am trying to make is that the time doesn't really matter in the whole scheme of things but it is however a marker to assess your progress and your direction of travel so don't dismiss it completely. I have an average 5K run time of about 34 minutes, but after coming back from having a baby I found myself back up to 46 minutes, and then in August 2014 while training for Tough Mudder and not even doing much running I managed a 30.07, now where the hell did that come from?

People often ask me what the average time is for someone running their first 5K: well in my experience it could be anything from 20 minutes to an hour and 20, so while you are still building up to being able to run consistently without stopping for those kind of times there is no harm in you getting used to being on your feet for a similar amount of time. One of the biggest fears about doing races is not being able to finish, but if you know you can at a bare minimum walk for an hour, there really isn't anything to worry about.

So in a nutshell this session is about going out for as long as you like…walking, jogging or running…don't come home until at least an hour has gone. Feel like a proper runner yet?

Week 3 - Improving Technique

Wow, we are on week 3 of the programme already how did that happen? You have ticked off 6 running sessions and we haven't once spoken about what to actually do with your legs nor mention how to control your breathing, well not in any detail anyway.

So let's talk technique.

Have you ever watched people running? Like really watched them? Once you start running yourself you will find that you do this all the time, desperate to find some common traits that you can implement yourself in the hope of seeing some improvement.

You will be amazed at how different they all look though, and in some cases you might think "how do they even run like that?" Probably people look at me and think the same but I don't really care…well not much anyway.

As discussed earlier in the book, the movement of your body when running is quite simple, even if it is quite hard. You pick up each leg alternatively, you swing your arms and you project yourself in a forward motion. That's it in a nutshell, so how come there is a whole industry based on things like GAIT analysis and biomechanical coaching (not sure that's even a term) but you know what I mean. You can't pick up a running book or magazine without someone harping on about how the positioning of your various joints can knock of 30 seconds each mile.

In my opinion though an over emphasis of technique in the early days of running can actually hinder your progress. I would say for at least the first 6 months or so you should focus on creating a habit of running, a desire to run, an aptitude for it. Over analysis of where you are going wrong can just be negative and make you feel like you are getting it all wrong, besides simply by improving your fitness you are likely to see great improvements anyway.

But there are a few things technique wise you can integrate from the start, simple things, which should give you a bit of added confidence and possibly even accelerated progress, the ones we are going to focus on all impact on each other and all begin with the letter P, just to make it easy for you to remember.

- Panting
- Posture
- Pace

I believe that over and above any other advice around technique, by focusing on these 3 you are more likely to see improvements in the early stages of your running…and they are all things that you can implement easily. So every time you go for a run think to yourself am I doing my 3 P's?

Lets have a look at them in more detail?

Panting

Getting your breathing right is tough, there's no two ways about it, and this is heightened at the start of your running journey when you are self conscious, unfit and a bit panicky about the whole thing, it's no wonder your breathing is all over the place.

Sometimes it comes as a bit of a shock as we realise that we are unfit, or simply we are embarrassed by the panting noises we make. In my opinion, if you are making noises, it means you are working hard and that's what we want.

Our breathing only really becomes difficult when we find ourselves running a little faster than our body can cope with, because after all the basic reason for breathing is to send oxygen to the muscles we are using. But we will talk more about pace in a while. The first race I ever did I went off like a shot trying to keep up with everyone else and literally within 30 seconds I had to stop due to the burning sensation in my windpipe and my ability to catch my breath and I can still wind myself too early in the final sprint of a run if I'm not careful.

So how do we solve this problem?

Task 11 – Deep breathing practice

We need to breathe properly and that requires a bit of practice. Lay down on the floor for a moment…yep now will do (unless you are reading this on your kindle on the train). Place your hands on your abdomen and breath. Try to locate where the air is going, is it going to your lungs and boobs or your tummy? It should be your tummy. Practice for a bit lying down, breathing slow and deeply using your diaphragm the more you can control this when up and running the less likelihood you will suffer from stitches which are caused by muscle spasms in that area.

The first run of the week in week 3 is all about listening to your breathing and trying to regulate it using deep breathing. One way of assessing how well you are doing is via the talk test, can you talk in short bursts (if so you are running at about the right pace for you) if not you are running too fast. If you are able to hold a full blown conversation, then you are not working hard enough.

Posture

In general, many of us runners, or in fact non-runners, could do with standing up just a little bit taller. Just think how much slimmer and more confident we would look for a start. You know that thing you do when you pose for a picture? Sucking in your gut, rolling our shoulders back and smiling. How is it that we can adjust our body to be photographed in an instant but 90% of the time we slouch and slump and make things that much harder for ourselves?

Aside from improving your appearance, keeping your posture in check when running is going to prevent a number of things

1. Aches and pains
2. Stiches
3. Slumps in confidence
4. Fatigue

And it should make you lighter on your feet and more able to push yourself. But how do you know how to hold yourself? Well I do something called a top to toe test. I picked this up as a teenager when for one summer I was part of a modeling troupe…I will never forget the camp catwalk coach screaming at me "walk with your fanny luv, walk with your fanny" in an attempt to get me leading from the hips as I sashed from one side of a sports hall to another practicing our routine.

I revisited a similar technique after having my daughter when I realised the pushing of a pram and the carrying of her on the same hip was wreaking havoc with the way I held myself, all slouched and lopsided.

Task 12 – Top to toe assessment

The second task of this week is one about correcting your form, or at least testing it out. Head out for 20 minutes or longer if you can manage it, but keep your mind occupied with the following process.

The top to toe test

Head – Smile (or at least don't grimace) imagine a string pulling your head towards the sky and an apple under your chin so you don't look down. Your eyes should be focused on the horizon, not fixed to the pavement looking out for dog poo.

Shoulders – Roll them back and give them a few shrugs, make sure they don't creep up towards your ears as you run, continue to roll them back to release tension and stress.

Boobs – Be proud of your bad boys, don't push them out and don't suck them in, and whatever you do don't use your arms to try and control them…get a good sports bra for that.

Arms – Let them hang loose, don't hold any tension in your fingers so no fist clenching. Let them swing like a pendulum and only pump them if you want or need to up your pace…you know like if you are being chased by a tiger!!

Tummy – Hold it in, but don't hold your breath. Imagine you have put your jeans on and are tightening up your belt, don't tighten it all the way up just a little tighter than it usually is.

Hips – The technical term is hip extension which is all to do with the best positioning to enable forward motion, think running with your fanny, rather than sticking your bum out (sorry that's the best way I can describe it).

Legs – Just keep them moving as naturally as you can, the longer you can stay in the air between strides the better.

Feet – Land on your foot in the position which feels most comfortable, lift them a little of the ground to ensure you don't trip but not too much it drains your energy.

Did you know that side stitches are found to occur more frequently in runners that slouch over or hunch their backs while running. The poorer the running posture, the more severe the side stitches reported.

Pace

One of the biggest complaints I receive from female runners is about pace or more to the point their lack of it. "Oh but I'm just so slow" or "I just can't run fast" which I don't believe at all. Everyone can run faster in the early days of their running it just takes a bit of effort…most of us are just too scared to try it or to admit to ourselves that we don't put in enough effort to see results.

But speed isn't everything, especially when you are just starting out. We are focusing on being able to run or run/walk a 5k and it doesn't matter what time you do this in, it doesn't matter in the slightest.

Rather than thinking about running fast as a beginner you want to concentrate on running slow, like I mean REALLY slow, almost slow enough that a walker might overtake you. Seriously. This simulated slow motion running is going to really help you build up your capacity to run for longer periods of time and build up your confidence.

There is one exception to this, and that is when you are doing intervals.

Task 13 – Experimenting with speed

For this session you will need a watch, it doesn't have to be a stopwatch unless you want to be super accurate. You will need to allocate 30 minutes and find yourself somewhere to run where you are unlikely to be disturbed by traffic or pedestrians etc, a park with loops can be good so too could a running track, if you are brave enough. After a short warm up, I want you to break your running up into 5 blocks, for 4 minutes you will run at normal plodding speed but for one minute you will go full blast running as hard as you can. Now if you are not at the stage that you can run consistently for 4 minutes then break the sessions down to one or two minute blocks, use the slower bits to recover and save a few minutes at the end to cool down and stretch.

Week 4 - Be Inspired

Remember how at the start of this book we talked about finding your personal motivation for starting up running, finding your very own WHY!! Well with 3 weeks training under our belt we are going to come back to that idea, because it's possible that the novelty of becoming a runner is starting to wear thin. All those social occasions you have to turn down, the episodes of Corrie you have to catch up on…and let's not mention the increase in dirty laundry you now have to do.

It would be so easy now to fall back into bad habits, or perhaps even delay your 5k race, because you feel you haven't progressed as much as you would have liked to. But hang on a moment, you are 4 weeks into a 5-week programme, how the hell are you going to quit now when you are so close?

What you need to do now to keep your motivation high is to find the fun in your running, to mute those negative voices and to look for inspiration in some new surroundings.

So this chapter is going to explore

- Routes
- Music

When I first started running, I used to have 3 basic routes, two of which that were quite secluded so that I couldn't be seen or heckled, and all of them within a 3-mile radius of my home. It's no wonder I found it hard to run regularly…my running was boring me to tears; there was no real incentive for me to lace up my shoes, nothing to excite me about leaving out the front door each week.

Signing up to races helped a little with my motivation, but this sometimes meant I ran more races in a year than I ran training sessions…which, as you can imagine, left we feeling frustrated with my race times and my ability to run them strongly, and not to mention the expense of doing regular races or the havoc it played on my social life.

When I joined a running club (6 years after first starting running I might add), the having to choose my own route problem kind of stopped, as someone else in the club had that job and I simply had to turn up and do as I was told each week. But even then the routes, despite being changed frequently, were still not that inspiring.

But then one day I realised I could simply plot my own; it dawned on me that I could actually run wherever I wanted to and I didn't need to stick to the routes near where I lived either…I could drive somewhere nice, jump on a train and go somewhere else where nobody would know me which, at the time, was a huge added bonus. One day, when buying some new running shoes, I spotted a book by the till called "25 London Runs" and added it to my order. That book inspired me to finally explore the city I had lived in my whole life, opening up so many possibilities for training routes and giving me the confidence to branch out from my comfort zone. I still have a few suggestions to try from that book if ever I run out of ideas.

Task 14 – Plot a new route

So this task is simple, you just need to run somewhere new, somewhere you haven't run before. Think about where you have been running so far on this challenge: is it rural or is it in the middle of a city: are there loads of people around or is it reasonably quiet? What kind of route would you like to run in, what kind of surroundings are most likely to inspire you?

I once did a 7 mile run in St Lucia (yep you read that right) with a local lad who was willing to run with me to a place called Pigeon Island; it was the stand out moment of my holiday and possibly even my running career...we left the hotel at 5.30am in the morning so as to avoid the heat and I saw parts of the island I never would have as a tourist...and at the time my normal running distance was closer to 3 or 4 miles so it was tough, really tough. As you can imagine, I was a real spectacle for the local people, and that guy probably still tells the story of the time he accompanied a fat slow red faced tourist on a run around the island.

Now I am not for a minute suggesting you fly off somewhere exotic to find a new and exciting running route, but why not look at where you live and where you can get to within an hour that feels quite exciting. Is there a country park, a lake, a forest etc, perhaps ask some friends about the areas they live in or do some research online, there are many running websites which will suggest routes uploaded by other runners and even a few mobile phone apps.

So while we are on that point, do you run with your phone? Do you use it for music perhaps? I have to admit I have never really cracked the what to listen to music wise while running. For a while, I had a playlist called Running Tunes, which consisted mainly of cheesy 80s and 90s music, think MJ and the Spice Girls, but I soon got bored of that. Part of my problem is that I didn't really have a view on what would inspire me, and the other problem is that I am often too lazy to be bothered to plan it...this lead me once to running a 10K race with the soundtrack to Les Miserables...I ran the last few miles of that in silence as it was driving me mad…but then the voices in my head were doing a pretty good job of that too.

I would say that runners listen to music for 4 main reasons

1. To break up the monotony of the session
2. To help with pacing
3. To be inspired
4. To drown out the negative voices in their head

But I have found that music isn't always successful in all of those, well not for me at least and too frequently I have ended up having a full blow argument with myself mid training run about what to listen to and blaming my terrible run session on the fact I have been listening to the wrong music.

That was until I discovered podcasts.

The first podcast I started listening to was one called Marathon Talk, which as you can guess is all about the sport of Marathon running, now I am not for a minute suggesting you listen to that one, in fact, I would suggest you don't…obviously for me listening to an hour of experts talking about the sport was beneficial due to where I was in the development of my business, in fact I later went on to be interviewed as a guest on the show…but I reckon if you listened to it at the stage you are at now, it might well scare you off.

You need to think about what you are personally going to find motivating.

Task 15 – Podcast/Audiobook Run

What you need to do is find a topic that you are interested in, one that is going to stimulate your mind and give you something to think about rather than thinking about how tough the running is, or how long you still have to run.

There are so many free podcasts available on every topic you can think of…running, fitness, diet, psychology….but also less serious ones voiced by celebrities like Stephen Fry, Ricky Gervais etc so find something that works for you. You may decide that audiobooks are better for you, and the same rules apply, make the book something you will want to listen to something which is going to prompt you to put your running trainers on time and time again.

This task is simple…get something new to listen to and head out for a 30 minute run, unless you want to run for longer. But beware your longest run is coming up this weekend so don't go mad. When you get home from this session have a think about how different it felt: if you were able to run for longer or even run faster.

So now you know…there is a long run coming up this weekend. Probably the longest run you are going to do in this 5-week challenge. But what do I mean by long?

When you first start out a long run could be a mile, when you are marathon training a long run is anything from 17 to 22 miles and is likely to take the majority of the day…well it does for me.

I can remember when I was training for my first full marathon in 2012, I had left the house at 8am and at 2pm my partner phoned and said "Where the hell are you?" in a voice of panic. I was at about mile 15 and about a mile away from home. I had been plodding around East London oblivious to how long I had been out for, and I had stopped a few times to refuel and stretch etc. so I could see why he was a little concerned.

But whether you are training for a marathon or for a 5K the principles of doing your longest training run are pretty much the same.

- You have to mentally prepare
- You have to fuel yourself right
- You need to know where you are running
- You need to be organized and take everything you may need
- You need to have mini milestones to break it up
- You need a route which is going to inspire you

Well this is how I cope with clocking up those miles

Task 16 – Sightseeing Run

You have some experience of planning new routes now, and hopefully your earlier run this week will have taken you out of your comfort zone a little and got you used to running in new surroundings. This task is going to take that to a new level though.

I want you to choose a route, somewhere reasonably local to you, that is known for its natural beauty or its potential for sightseeing opportunities. I need you to plan a route which is likely to take you an hour or so…YES an HOUR or so…you read that right.

But do not fear, I am not expecting you to be able to run the whole of it, but I do expect you to complete the route and get used to being on your feet for that amount of time.

The purpose of this training run is to give you confidence that you can finish the 5K event, but, more important than that, the uniqueness of the route and the way you approach this training run will hopefully show you that running doesn't have to be about speed and distance.

I am lucky to live in East London on the outskirts of the Queen Elizabeth Olympic Park. This is the area that the London 2012 Olympic and Paralympic games were held, and 3 years on what is left is beautiful parklands with winding canals, modern art and of course the spectacular venues so often my runs feel like they are sightseeing runs. But I am also known to jump on a tube and do a few laps of Hyde Park, taking pictures of the famous statues and monuments along the course. One of my other favorite routes is also along the Thames which although is quite challenging due to the number of pedestrians, nothing can beat the buzz of seeing all those iconic tourist landmarks.

As you make your way around your chosen route, really look at your surroundings; notice the way the clouds look, the scenic views and the architecture. Stop to take some photos and upload them to your social media sites. If you need to take a break and rest your feet for a while do, but never for more than a few minutes…perhaps do some stretches and take on some water before heading off again.

For an hours worth of running you won't really need to refuel on the go, but perhaps a few sweeties in your back pocket or a small box of raisins just in case you feel like you need a little sugar fix towards the end.

Ladies, you are nearly there. You have come so far on this programme, and the last task marked the toughest session of them all, so congratulations on getting to this point.

Week 5 – Believing you can do it

So as we enter this final week I have a few question for you.

At this point do you believe you can run that 5K? Do you think you have done enough training? Basically with a week to go do you think you can do it?

I bet you can even if you don't think you can.

Even if you are not 100% confident about completing it, are you at least surprised at the progress you have made recently? Or are you still being plagued by those bloody negative voices that continue to tell you that you can't do it. I thought you would have got them under control by now, although I admit I still allow mine to surface some times.

Those negative voices in your head never completely disappear, you just get better at managing them (ie switching them off) the more experienced you become.

There are a few other ways of switching the mind on to a new more positive, constructive way of thinking, and that is what we are going to focus on this week…oh and a little bit of gentle exercise to make sure you are nice and loose for the big day.

Task 17 – What's the worst that can happen?

We've all been there right? You have a big occasion coming up, a test, a social event, a presentation at work, you do all the preparation needed you feel confident and then you let in a "but what if…." thought and before you know if your mind is bombarded with them. So rather than push these o the back of your head I want you to list them. Now remember this is specifically in relation to the running of your 5k this weekend. So it may include things like

- What if I wake up late on the day?
- What if I don't get a good night sleep?
- What if I am unwell?
- What if my nerves get the better of me?
- What if I arrive late to the start line?
- What if I am too nervous to eat?
- What if I feel sick at the start line?
- What if I fall over during the race?
- What if I go off too quick?
- What if I am last

Now ladies this list can go on and on, and quite often it does so let yourself really go for it and don't stop until you have absolutely exhausted all of the things you are worried about.

Now what?

Well, now we are going to plan to eliminate the potential risk and then after that we play the "So what?" game again.

So for example

What if I wake up late on the day. Well firstly I am going to go to bed early, I will set 2 alarms and I will get a friend to call me 5 minutes after I am supposed to be awake. But if none of that happens, so what if I wake up late? It would be disappointing, and I might have to rush around, I might even miss it completely. But the likelihood of that happening is very small so perhaps I shouldn't worry about this too much after all.

Do you see how this could be useful?

So go through your complete list and think about how to minimize risk, look at the risk in terms of its likelihood in the first place and then assess the damage if that risk actually ended up happening.

This is a great way of illuminating fears but also more importantly getting you prepared and focused on the event.

Task 18 – Lets keep those legs loose (combine this with task 21)

With all this talk about the race you might be tempted to get another big session in. NO. That's the worst thing you could do. But I do want you to run this week, just the once. But it must be a very light easy run. An out and back jog or powerwalk of 15 minutes there and back. Whilst out there, think about how far you have come and how strong you feel. Take note of how your body feels and know that it will feel even stronger on race day. Make sure you give yourself a good stretch when you get home after this your final training session.

Task 19 – How does it feel?

So you are an athlete now, you do know that right? You run regularly, you follow a training plan, you sign up for events…you even do a bit of sports psychology, so in my books you are an athlete.

Now I want you to set aside 20 minutes somewhere quiet and think about what this actually means. You might feel a bit weird doing this but it is important, so take it seriously and make this happen.

Lay down, on the couch or on your bed…the floor will do too. Make sure everything is switched off, the TV, the radio, your mobile phone. Choose a time when everyone else is out of the house or asleep.

Take 20 minutes to think about how you feel when you run, how strong you feel and how great it feels to achieve something that many people find difficult. Visualize yourself as that strong powerful athlete that will achieve the goals you have set out for yourself.

If any negative thoughts come in to your mind, push them away and replace them with something more positive, images of you at the start line feeling confident, or you crossing the finish line happy.

Task 20 - Give your legs a treat

In a few days time you will be giving your 5k event the best you can, and to get to the start line in tip top condition you want to give your legs a little bit of a rest. After all they have been through a lot over the last 5 weeks.

So here are a few ideas for treating them

- Book in a sports massage - tell the therapist when you are racing so they apply the right pressure.
- Have a pedicure – visit a salon or do it at home but be sure to get your toe nails cut right down and leave at least 2 or 3 days before the big day
- Foot massage – Get your partner to massage your toes, or use a tennis ball and some firm pressure to massage the underneath of each foot
- Stretch it out – A bit of light yoga or some gentle stretching will help prepare your legs
- Hair Removal – I doubt you will be baring your legs so this is not for aerodynamic purposes, but just for pampering properties and relaxation.

- Moisturize – Exfoliate and then slap on your favorite moisturizing cream and spend 20 minutes or so rubbing it into your pins.

Task 21 – Give us a fashion show

Decide on what you are going to wear on race day and give it a little test run of at least half of the distance to make sure it is not going to cause any problems on the day.

Race Day Preparation

Despite the apprehension we all have in the lead up to big races I often say that getting to the start line is the hardest part of any race. The fact that you committed to this event in the first place, when many don't, is amazing and the hours you have given up to the training needs to be congratulated.

Some of the information below about racing may not completely apply to you. Perhaps your 5k event is something you are doing alone and more of a personal challenge. Or maybe you are running your 5K with a small group of friends or taking part in something like parkrun, but many of the tips for racing apply to preparing for your first big distance event anyhow.

Taking part in a running race can be THE most amazing experience, however it can also be incredibly stressful with the potential for so much to go wrong. When you are a larger lady or someone new to the sport somehow the list of things that could go wrong increases too or maybe its just the fear of it all going wrong that increases. But by following some simple guidelines you can help make the whole day run smoother for both yourself and your biggest supporters, so that you can concentrate on just enjoying the race.

Things to remember

It is only a race. You may have trained hard, it may have been a big step for you to do it in the first place and you might have sacrificed a whole heap to get to the start line, but try not to blow it out of perspective...it is only a running event.

There will be other races in the future hopefully. Keep your eyes and ears open and absorb as much as your can both from others around you but also in terms of how you personally cope in this environment, you can use this information to prepare for next time.

It is supposed to be fun as well as being part of your fitness journey or raising money for charity you should also set yourself the goal of enjoying it, smile, take pictures, make friends and soak up the atmosphere, it will be over before you know it.

Race packs are normally sent out 2-3 weeks before the race day. Make sure you read it carefully and make notes about the important logistics like timings and travel directions. Take time to look at the route and consider a race plan. Look at where the water stops are or turning points. Start to visualise yourself running the course and finishing it in style.

In the days leading up to your event hydrate, hydrate, hydrate or in other words drink water until you are sick of the stuff and do not eat anything unusual in the days leading up. Include some carbohydrate (rice, pasta, potatoes, bread) in each of your meals but do not go overboard. Steer clear of alcohol all together

Get yourself organised with all of your kit and lay it out in the room you are going to get ready in. Write your emergency details on the back of your race number and agree on an emergency plan with your loved ones, what to do if you do not complete the race or you get lost at the end

Consider what time you would like to finish and then set yourself a best case and worse case scenario time, this will help you to stay strong if anything goes wrong. Go over the logistics one more time. Study the weather forecast, check for road closures or any last minute changes to public transport and know exactly how you plan to get to the start line. If you are feeling a bit edgy go for a brisk walk to loosen up

The night before, do everything within your power to conserve your energy and stay calm. Have a relaxing bath and stretch. Set an alarm early enough so that you do not have to rush. Switch off all electrical goods at least an hour before going to bed. Ask someone to give you a call shortly after your alarm to check you are up. Attempt an early night, but if you have trouble sleeping, write down what is worrying you and then try again. Finally…visualise how great you will feel this time tomorrow night

On the morning of your run have a good breakfast at least 2 hours before you are due to race and start to hydrate as soon as you wake. Make your way to the start line leaving yourself at least an hour before the start. Only take what you absolutely need with you, if you can travel light enough not to have to use the bag drop then even better

Carry an extra layer to keep you warm if you need to, an old t-shirt that you don't mind throwing away or plastic bin bag which will help keep you warm if it is windy or raining. Touch base with your loved ones and reiterate your emergency plan

When you arrive at the event location remember to stay calm and try to watch what everyone else is doing. Join the queue for the toilets even if you don't feel like you need to go. Take part in the warm up, if not do some dynamic stretches on your own. Make your way to the start with at least 15 minutes to spare. Talk to others at the start this will help with nerves. Be careful of your footing as you approach the starting line as there may be plastic bags, bottles and clothes.

As you cross the starting line take a deep breath and smile. Take in the atmosphere and remember all of the techniques you have learned over the last few weeks. Remember panting, posture and pace and don't forget you have the 60-second rule if you really need it. The race will be over before you know it.

As you sprint across the finish line congratulate yourself for what you have just done. Enjoy the moment, soak it all in.

In all the excitement it is easy to forget that you need to drink to rehydrate yourself. But you will also want to make the most of the atmosphere too.

Task 22 - Take a picture

Of you and your medal many of us forget to do this, or feel to shy to ask a stranger…you will regret not capturing this moment.

Pick up your bag if you left one in the bag drop and add a layer/remove wet clothes ASAP. Head to your agreed meeting point to reacquaint yourself with family, or if you are alone find someone else like you and congratulate them.

Eat something in the first half an hour like a banana or a cereal bar, and then something substantial as soon as possible after that. Try to remember to stretch.

But most of all enjoy the feeling of being a winner

Conclusion

When we started out on this journey together we spent some time looking at the fears so many of us let take over our lives, but now 5 weeks down the line you have achieved something that many people never have the courage to even contemplate.

OK so perhaps you didn't run the whole way, maybe you walked most of it and felt disappointed by your time but none of that even matters, the main thing we are celebrating the fact you made a commitment to try something out of your comfort zone, you followed a programme and you gave it your all…we never expected anything more than that.

So revel in the excitement of what you have achieved, how great you felt as you crossed that line, those moments of sheer enjoyment as you made your way round the course should keep you motivated moving forward. These are most definitely things to celebrate.

Take a few days to absorb how you feel about the whole process before you dissect the event too harshly, but by all means think about the things you could have done better…but instead frame it within a "this is how I am going to improve for next time"

One of the biggest mistakes new runners make after their first event is they say NEVER AGAIN and go back to their sedentary lifestyles, especially if their 5K was about proving something to someone, or raising money for a specific charity close to their heart.

But you guys have not only been training to run a 5-kilometre race, you have been learning to love the sport of running. So somewhere deep inside a seed has been planted and hopefully you will want to go back out and train. Perhaps you will want to focus on maintaining your running habit or maybe you (like me) need a race in the diary to help keep you motivated, either way don't leave it too long before going out for a run.

Task 23 – Schedule your next run

It doesn't have to be a long run, but a few days later take your legs out for a bit of a spin and see how different you feel now you have conquered that goal. An out and back for 10 minutes will be plenty but do run more if you feel up to it. Remember to listen to your body.

This book is not just a simple couch to 5k programme that gets you to that final destination and then leaves you destitute. Many of the challenges featured in the plan can be applied time and time again, so don't chuck away that checklist just yet. Some of you may feel ready to progress to a bigger distance or even to join a running club, but many of you will feel like you still have some unfurnished business with this distance. So why not jump straight back in from the beginning and see how much stronger you can become in the next 5 weeks.

It took me a good few years to understand that my running was only ever going to improve once I started training properly and being more consistent in all aspects of my lifestyle.

Task 24 – Set some new goals

Reviewing progress and setting new goals is an integral part of being an athlete and it is what is likely to keep you inspired by the sport. Finding a way of being accountable to your goals is also important too. This could be by joining a running club or simply hanging out in a Facebook page for runners. Check out www.facebook.com/thefatgirlsguidetorunning

List 4 or 5 things you are going to move forward with as a result of achieving this goal, pin it to somewhere where you will see it every day and perhaps tell some friends so that you remain accountable.

Running is a very diverse sport in as much as you have elite runners like the ones we see on the TV, the people like us and also lots of types in between. I don't like giving anyone a title, as we are all unique in terms of our dreams and aspirations, who wants to be known as a beginner or as joggers or newbies, I even find the term club runner quite useless because we are all simply just runners at different stages in our running journey.

The trick with progressing in this sport and feeling like you are part of the wider running community is to stand up and be counted. Get engaged in the debate online, talk to other runners if you get the opportunity or simply smile as you pass each other on the streets. The only way we are ever going to feel like one big happy family as runners is to accept that we are all different and to celebrate that difference with our shared love of running bonding us together.

I hope this book and the journey you have been on to reach the 5k mark has opened your eyes to the various aspects of running, not only in terms of the physical requirements, but also the mental strength you need and the trickery you can employ to keep those negative voices away.

5 Kilometers is a great distance to build up to and away from and as runners there are few of us that will leave that distance behind in our training. Once you crack being able to run for 5k

without stopping your confidence will soar and you will have so many more options for taking it to the next step.

Running has absolutely changed my life over the last 10 years and enabled me to do things I never thought possible. When I tie my shoes up and close the front door behind me, I am not just going out for a run, I am making a statement, I am rewarding myself with some me time and I am showing that exercise can and should be enjoyed by everyone...even those of us who don't look like traditional runners.

I was given these legs for a reason, and it sure as hell wasn't just to look good in high heels, although these days they kind of are, even if I do say so myself.

Thank you for coming on this journey with me and good luck in all of your running endeavors.

And just before you leave us

Task 25 – This is a little bit of a cheeky one....

If you have read this book and found it useful then why not tell other women just like you about it, why not leave a review on Amazon about the bits that really helped you.

If you would like to support the Fat Girls Guide to Running further while at the same time develop your confidence as a runner you could consider one of the following

1. Join the Clubhouse – this is our virtual running club, which helps women to be more accountable, develop in speed and distance and find their love of running.
2. Buy one of our Technical Tee Shirts so that you are spotted at events, or on training runs. They often

prompt over women to consider taking up running so by wearing one you act as a role model
3. Take part in #OneBigFatRun our FREE virtual 5K which takes place on the last Sunday of every month.

Run strong, run happy

Check List

Task 1	Sign up to a 5K race
Task 2	The first attempt out and back 10
Task 3	Letting it all out
Task 4	Play the "so what?" game
Task 5	Out and back for 12
Task 6	Out and back for 15
Task 7	Baseline Record
Task 8	The Getaway
Task 9	How long can you last?
Task 10	Time on your feet test
Task 11	Deep breathing practice
Task 12	Top to toe assessment
Task 13	Experimenting with speed
Task 14	Plot a new route
Task 15	Podcast/Audiobook Run
Task 16	Sightseeing Run
Task 17	What's the worst that can happen?
Task 18	Lets keep those legs loose
Task 19	How does it feel?

Task 20   Give your legs a treat

Task 21   Give us a Fashion Show

Task 22   Take a photo with your Medal

Task 23   Schedule and complete your next run

Task 24   Set some new goals

Task 25   Help promote The Fat Girls Guide to Running

Acknowledgements

I first started writing about my running experiences after coming last in a 10K race in 2010, the fact I came last was embarrassing enough but realizing they had packed away the finish line and water stations too took that embarrassment to a whole new level and a few hours later The Fat Girls Guide to Running blog was formed.

At that point I had no idea that it would grow to what it has, or change my life like is has but I did know somehow that I just had to speak out about what it felt like to be overweight and pretty much a rubbish runner trying to make their way in the mainstream running community, never in a million years though did I imagined how it would touch so many people.

Recently I received the following message that kind of sums it all up

"I literally cried when I found your page…thank you for using the word "fat" …thank you for making me think there is a possibility that I am allowed to be fat and enjoy exercise. Most of all…thank you for letting me know that I don't have to be myself by myself!

Over the last 4 years I have been blessed that so many runners have opened up their experiences with me, shared their insecurities and prompted me to find solutions for them, I haven't done this alone. I have had an awful lot of support from the ladies who follow my blog, ladies who have bought merchandise from me, booked onto my one day retreats, offered to proof read things and turn up with very little notice for media things.

We all know how wonderful women are when they pull together and support one another, so I just want to take this opportunity to thank you all. I am driven to make things better for women because so many women over the years have made things better for me.

A few years ago I went to see a local business advisor to get some support to turn my blog into an enterprise, he told me in no uncertain terms that the blog was a hobby not a business, and that it was all about my ego. A few weeks later a female business coach spent a day with me helping me to map things out and within a fortnight I had launched a new website, merchandise line and speaking business.

It is often said when one woman wins we all win, so get out there and achieve your goals and then share those successes with the women you know and then the women you don't.

If you enjoyed this book and think it would help other women you know or don't know, tell them about it either in person or via social media, and if you really like it why not leave me a review on Amazon about how it has helped you...cos that's what its all about really

I am on a mission to get 1 million women running in the UK, and do you know even then there will still be 1 million more men in the country playing sport than their female counterparts...we still have a long way to go.

Happy Running

THE CLUBHOUSE

Are you a plus size runner struggling to find your way? Do you lack motivation with your running or even the know how to reach your goals? Would you like the support of an awesome community of women just like you and of course the opportunity to be coached by the author of this eBook Julie Creffield?

The Clubhouse is the worlds first Virtual Running Club for Plus Sized women, in fact you don't even need to be overweight its simply an inclusive place for runners of all shapes and sizes, and more importantly levels of ability to celebrate their joy of running.

For more information about how to join check out www.toofattorun.co.uk/the-clubhouse

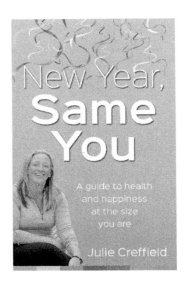

Are you worried about making and breaking yet another New Years resolution related to your dwindling health and fitness? Or will this year be the year where you finally stick to your diet, persevere with the gym and get the body of your dreams? Who you kidding? Well what if I told you there was a more effective way of finding balance, and achieving health and fitness goals that don't rely on that sure to fail all or nothing approach.

New Year, Same You shows you how it is possible to find balance too by taking away the pressure be anyone other than yourself. Because ladies, guess what? You are already enough.

Available in paperback and kindle from [Amazon](#) and you don't have to read it at the start of a new year either.

Are you ready to take you running up a notch and commit to a 10K race? Well this simple eBook gives you all the techniques and know how you will need to prepare for this distance, and gives you the confidence to commit to achieving this in just 10 weeks.

Available to download from <u>Amazon</u> for less than the price of a Big Mac meal.

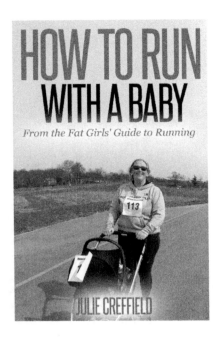

Are you a busy mum? Do you struggle to find the time or motivation to exercise? This eBook gives you 99 suggestions for how to integrate fitness into your busy life as an awesome mum, and without the guilt or fear we often experience. Taking you from newborn right up to having adult children, this book covers all the bases and helps you to encourage a culture of activity in your home.

Available to download from <u>Amazon</u> for less than the price of a Chicken in a box meal.

Printed in Great
Britain
by Amazon